The Pittsburgh, Pennsylvania

Bucket List

Susan B. Malcolm, Ph.D.

Peggy.

Thank you so much for including me in your grand opening festivities! all the best.

Susan Malcolm

The Pittsburgh, Pennsylvania

Bucket List

Susan B. Malcolm, Ph.D.

The Pittsburgh, Pennsylvania Bucket List /
Susan B. Malcolm, Ph.D.

ISBN-13: 9781499520705
ISBN-10: 1499520700

Acknowledgements

Thank you to my husband Tom and my children Jim, Megan, and Sarah Schultz and my parents, Suzanne and James Malcolm, who offered ideas and support during the evolution of the book. Special thanks to my mom, Suzanne, who is my professional proofreader.

Thank you to Eli Carrington, graphic designer with Blur Graphics, who was instrumental in selecting appropriate images and icons that are used throughout the book. His patience and professionalism during the process was appreciated.

Thank you to *The Bucket List of Ocean City New Jersey* author Mary Ann Bolan, and her husband Bob Bolan, for supporting this effort and simplifying the project.

Legal Disclaimer

This book is designed to provide information, entertainment, and motivation to readers. It is sold with the understanding that the publisher is not engaged to render any type of physical, psychological, legal, or any other kind of advice. Participation in some of the activities may be dangerous and could lead to serious injury or death. The content of this book is the sole expression and opinion of its author and not necessarily that of the publisher. No warranties or guarantees are expressed or implied. Neither the publisher nor the individual author shall be liable for any physical, psychological, emotional, financial, or commercial damages, including, but not limited to, special, incidental, consequential, or other damages. Readers are responsible for choices, actions, and resulting outcomes.

About the Author

Susan B. Malcolm worked in business and consulting for 20 years and simultaneously started teaching at Robert Morris University. After having a family, and in need of schedule flexibility, Susan pursued her M.S. Ed. and Ph.D., and focused on research and teaching. While working at Duquesne University, Susan was fortunate enough to spend an academic year in Rome in 2010-11 and to subsequently work with student debaters. She has since moved to Robert Morris University where she teaches communication classes.

The Pittsburgh, Pennsylvania
Bucket List

The Pittsburgh, Pennsylvania Bucket List offers a snapshot of Pittsburgh; places that attract newcomers and entertain residents. This assembly of things to do and places to go form a paradoxical portrait of Pittsburgh that blends industrial tradition with technological innovation, ethnic neighborhoods with integrated communities, and loyal sports fans with cultural elite, in a city that is fluid but not finite.

The *Bucket List* includes a variety of places to go and things to do within and outside of the city limits. The contents provide newcomers with a starting point for seeing and experiencing Pittsburgh and provide residents with a reminder of why Pittsburgh is one of America's most livable cities.

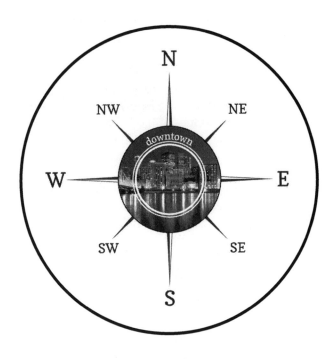

Downtown

Drive through the Fort Pitt tunnels at night toward the city of Pittsburgh.

A glittering city, nestled among three rivers, greets those who drive into Pittsburgh at night via Route 376 East and the Fort Pitt tunnels. This same scene captivated many in the 2010 film, "The Perks of Being a Wallflower" though standing in the back of a pick-up truck while driving is not recommended.

view

Where: Route 376 East from the Airport
                and Robinson Township toward
                Downtown

Web: www.pghbridges.com

Watch Pittsburgh awaken from one of the Mt. Washington overlooks.

Some of the most popular vantage points are from Mt. Washington overlooks. Early morning or after dark are primetime for clinching a parking spot along Grandview Avenue atop Mt. Washington. Multiple paths lead to this perch, including the Duquesne Incline from Station Square.

view

Where: Grandview Avenue
                Pittsburgh, PA

Web: www.tripadvisor.com/
                Attraction_Review-g53449-
                d272285-Reviews-Mount_
                Washington-Pittsburgh_
                Pennsylvania.html

Stroll at dawn across the Smithfield or 10th Street bridges.

Sunrise offers a hopeful beginning and watching the sunlight spread across the South Side slopes can be a calming way to start any day. The Smithfield and 10th Street bridges span the Monongahela River. The Smithfield extends from downtown to Station Square and the 10th Street bridge extends from Second Avenue to the South Side.

view

activity

Where: Multiple entry points
                Easiest to park at Station Square or
                the South Side to access the bridges.

Web: www.city.pittsburgh.pa.us/cp/
                maps/south_side_slopes.html

Mix it up with a land/river Ducky tour.

See Pittsburgh on land and water with a Ducky Tour that operates regularly from April 1 through October, and weekends during November. The adventure, in original WWII vehicles, is an hour long and moves on land and water. Tours start at Station Square and travel to various places throughout the city. Prices vary based upon age and reservations are recommended.

activity

Where: Just Ducky Tours
                125 West Station Square Drive
                Pittsburgh, PA 15219
                412-402-3825

Web: http://www.justduckytours.com/

Wander through downtown during Monday through Friday and spend time to appreciate the architectural blend of old and new buildings.

The Pittsburgh Renaissances I and II have replaced some of the old with the new but there are still many places that maintain the grandeur of an earlier time. The website might help to narrow the focus – potential stops include the Union Trust Building, Allegheny City-County Building, and the Omni William Penn. Newer construction includes PPG Place, Mellon Bank Tower, and the soon-to- be completed Tower at PNC Plaza.

activity

view

culture

Where: Multiple locations
              Buildings are located between Grant
              and Stanwix Streets

Web: www.phlf.org/downloads/
              whirlwind_tour_for_web.pdf

Seek PNC Broadway Across America theatre shows in the Pittsburgh Cultural District.

The PNC Broadway Across America series produces approximately six shows each year from November through May. The performances are held at the Benedum Center (former Stanley Theater) and the productions include recent Broadway shows. Student tickets are available.

culture

music

Where: Pittsburgh Cultural Trust
                803 Liberty Avenue
                Pittsburgh, PA 15222
                Administration: 412-471-6070
                Tickets: 412-456-6666

Web: www.trustarts.org/

Enjoy Civic Light Opera Broadway shows throughout the summer months.

The Civic Light Opera (CLO) started in 1946 and also offers Broadway musical shows at the Benedum Center from May – July. In addition, the CLO performs smaller cabaret productions at the Pittsburgh Cultural District's Theater Square complex. Discounted student tickets are available.

culture   food

Where: Civic Light Opera
               719 Liberty Avenue
               Pittsburgh, PA 15222
               412-281-3973

Web: www.pittsburghclo.org/

Encourage up-and-coming talent at the Pittsburgh Musical Theater.

Pittsburgh Musical Theater offers productions from October through May each year. Theater training, education, and outreach are available through the conservatory. The public shows are held at the Byham Theater in downtown Pittsburgh and conservatory training is located in the West End. Discounted student tickets are available for shows.

culture   music

Where: Pittsburgh Musical Theater
                101 Sixth Street (Byham shows)
                Pittsburgh, PA 15222
                412-456-6666

                327 S. Main Street (Conservatory)
                Pittsburgh, PA 15220

Web: www.pittsburghmusicals.com/

Listen to the music—the world-renowned Pittsburgh Symphony Orchestra.

The Pittsburgh Symphony (PSO) started in 1896 and, with a brief interruption, has continued offering classical musical experiences until the present day. Most performances are held at Heinz Hall during a season that typically operates from October through June annually. Summers are often reserved for global tours. Discounted student tickets are available.

culture

music

Where: Pittsburgh Symphony Orchestra
600 Penn Avenue
Pittsburgh, PA 15222
412-392-3311

Web: www.pittsburghsymphony.org/
pso_home/web/mission-statement

Relish the dance offered by the Pittsburgh Ballet Theater.

The Pittsburgh Ballet Theatre (PBT) offers regional, national, and international performances. For 45 years, PBT has showcased contemporary and traditional ballet performances. Shows are usually held from October through April annually and live musical accompaniment infuses the shows with additional talent. Discounted student tickets are available.

culture

music

Where: Pittsburgh Ballet Theatre
           2900 Liberty Avenue
           Pittsburgh, PA 15201-1500
           412-281-0360

Web: www.pbt.org

Pause for pampering at the Omni William Penn.

This luxury hotel has combines the grandeur of its' 1916 era beginning with the dynamic of present day. The elegant lobby, two tier grand ballroom, and afternoon tea, are situated alongside 597 comfortable guestrooms, expansive conference facilities, high speed Wi-Fi, and updated fitness facilities. The hotel is less than 20 miles from the airport and is within walking distance of shopping, restaurants and theaters.

activity

food

culture

Where: Omni William Penn
              530 William Penn Place
              Pittsburgh, PA 15219
              412-281-7100

Web: www.omnihotels.com

Relish the calm at century-old churches.

There are four primary historic churches in the downtown
Pittsburgh area, all within a mile of the U.S. Steel Tower.
Notable are the: Smithfield United Church of Christ with its'
80 foot aluminum steeple, First Presbyterian Church with 13
Tiffany Studio stained glass windows, Trinity Cathedral and
its' ancient burial grounds, and First English Evangelical
Lutheran Church with a 170 foot spire.

activity   culture

Where: Multiple locations
                Churches located between Grant
                and Sixth Streets

                Pittsburgh History & Landmarks
                Foundation – Suite 450
                100 West Station Square Drive
                Pittsburgh, PA 15219

Web: www.phlf.org

Attend the St. Patrick's Day parade and enjoy the local festivities in Market Square before, during, and after the event.

The Pittsburgh St. Patrick's Day Parade is the second largest in the country with more than 23,000 participants and approximately 150,000 onlookers. Participation is by invitation only but onlookers participate in their own way; some arrive early and some stay late. Refreshments and revelry are available at numerous establishments.

activity   food

Where: Starts at Liberty Avenue and 11th

Web: www.pittsburghirish.org/parade/

                www.pittsburghirish.org/
                parade/ pressrelease/index.htm

Run the 10k Great Race and the Pittsburgh Marathon.

The annual Great Race, held in September, attracts more than 16,000 people to the 5k and 10k events. There are also small runs for toddlers and fitness walks for those less active. Depending on the chosen distance, the race starts in Squirrel Hill or Oakland. Everyone ends on the same course for the final run into Point State Park.

The Pittsburgh Marathon, held each May, takes runners through the neighborhoods of Pittsburgh. A half marathon, marathon relay, kids marathon, 5k, and pet walk events are also featured on this festive day.

activity

Where:	Great Race starts: 10k - Frick Park & Beechwood Blvd. 5 k – Fifth Avenue & Atwood Street
	Marathon starts: Downtown near the Convention Center
Web:	http://www.rungreatrace.com/ http://www.pittsbrughmarathon.com

Enjoy a day, night, or weekend strolling through the exhibits and performances of the Three Rivers Arts Festival.

Artwork abounds for 10 days each June when the Dollar Bank Three Rivers Arts Festival occupies Point State Park and surrounding areas. The festival has been held since 1960, and is produced by the Pittsburgh Cultural Trust. It balances the desires of traditional and new audiences with "wow" factors. Music, food, and activities complement the artwork. Music and art are free.

culture   music   food

Where: Point State Park and Gateway Center near the intersection of Liberty Avenue, Stanwix Street, and Penn Avenue

Web: www.3riversartsfest.org/

Build a boat and see it float … or not. Be a part of the "Anything that Floats" race that occurs annually at the Three Rivers Regatta.

The Three Rivers Regatta has been a summer tradition in Pittsburgh since 1977. Powerboat races, prize money, BMX stunt shows, sand sculptors, musical shows, and fireworks are a few of the attractions. More than 500,000 people flock to Point State Park and the North Shore during the Fourth of July week. All events are free.

activity

food

music

Where: Point State Park and North Shore

Web: www.threeriversregatta.net

Watch with wonder as the official Pittsburgh Fourth of July fireworks display lights the skies.

The Fourth of July spectacle stops all traffic; cars on bridge spans around the city, boats that cruise the three rivers, and pedestrian traffic on Mt. Washington and elsewhere. The fireworks offer a fitting conclusion to the annual Three Rivers Regatta. Of course, for Pittsburghers who cannot wait for the once a year spectacular, the Pittsburgh Pirate baseball team offers post-game fireworks frequently throughout the season.

view

Where: Various points as noted
                Smithfield Street Bridge
                Liberty Bridge

Web: www.threeriversregatta.net

Stand at the bar and order fish and chips for lunch at the Original Oyster House in Market Square.

The Original Oyster House has been pleasing patrons for over 140 years. The place is an institution and has been named a historic site by the Pittsburgh History and Landmarks Foundation. The bar and restaurant started with oysters and beer and now offers an expansive menu of fish and seafood as well as souvenir mugs and T-shirts.

food

Where: Original Oyster House
20 Market Square
Pittsburgh, PA 15222
412-566-7925

Web: http://originaloysterhouse
pittsburgh.com/

Meet a friend at Macy's "under the clock" and then dine inside at the Tic Toc Restaurant.

The clock has been a historic meeting point in Pittsburgh for over 40 years. Having survived the surrounding commercial real estate transitions, the clock at the corner used to be synonymous with Kaufmann's, a flagship downtown department store. Despite the changes to the store, this downtown location offers a convenient spot to meet –prior to lunch at the Tic Toc Restaurant—or an afternoon stroll through the recently renovated Mellon Park.

shop

food

Where: Macy's
Corner of Fifth and Smithfield Sts.
400 Fifth Avenue
Pittsburgh, PA 15219
412-232-2000

Web: www1.macys.com

**Explore the city's nationalities via food festivals –
German, Italian, Irish, Greek.**

Pittsburgh has often been referred to as a "melting pot" of
ethnicities. The reference relates to its' former days as an
industrial city that employed thousands of new immigrants.
Pittsburgh still attracts newcomers to health care, education,
and technological organizations from around the world. This
intercultural fabric extends to the food served at festivals
around the city.

food culture music

Where/Web: Multiple locations

German
Penn Brewery - Oktoberfest
800 Vinial Street, Pittsburgh, PA 15212
412-237-9400 Year round
http://www.pennbrew.com/

Hofbrauhaus - Oktoberfest
2705 South Water St., Pittsburgh, PA 15203
412-224-2438   Year round
http://hofbrauhauspittsburgh.com/

Irish - September
Irish Food Festival
1000 Sandcastle Dr., West Homestead, PA   15120
September annually – 22+ years
www.pghirishfest.org

Italian – Late August
Little Italy Days – 12+ years
Liberty Avenue, Bloomfield, PA
http://littleitalydays.com/

Greek – August and May
Holy Trinity Greek Orthodox Church – 40+ years
985 Providence Boulevard, Pittsburgh, PA 15237
412-366-8700   Late August
http://www.holytrinitypgh.org/festival

St. Nicholas Greek Orthodox Cathedral – 52+ years
419 S. Dithridge Street, Pittsburgh, PA 15213
412-682-3866   May
http://stnickspgh.org

Participate in Pittsburgh Penguin hockey mania, or listen to the music, at the Consol Energy Center.

Consol Energy Center opened in 2010 and is the home for the Pittsburgh Penguins hockey team. Consol is also a common venue for concerts and other cultural events. Seating capacity is more than 18,400 for hockey; 19,000 for basketball; 14,500 for end stage concerts; and 19,700 for center stage concerts. The facility also offers four conference rooms and a variety of dining and refreshment options.

activity   music

Where: Consol Energy Center
1001 Fifth Avenue
Pittsburgh, PA 15219
412-642-1800
1-800-745-3000

Web: www.consolenergycenter.com

Glean some insight about the city with a visit to the Senator John Heinz History Center in the Strip District.

The Heinz History Center tells the story of Pittsburgh origins in the context of a broader American history. The museum offers six floors of permanent and changing exhibits and it is affiliated with the Smithsonian Institution. Pittsburgh's role in the world is honored through long-term exhibits that recognize the first commercial radio station, the polio vaccine, the ferris wheel, and Western Pennsylvania sports tradition.

activity

culture

Where: Senator John Heinz History Center
           1212 Smallman Street
           Pittsburgh, PA 15222
           412-454-6000

Web: www.heinzhistory center.org

Shop the "Strip District" on Saturday morning—close to a holiday if you like the bustle.

This section is notorious as the former wholesale produce section of the city. Early hours, fresh products, local flavor, and bustling customers are characteristic of "The Strip." In addition to independent kiosks, a few of the Strip favorites include:

- breakfast at De Luca's (arrive early)
- coffee at La Prima Espresso or Prestogeorg Coffee Roasting Company
- biscotti at Enrico Biscotti Company
- Italian specialties at Pennsylvania Macaroni
- fish from Wholey's Market
- lunch at Primanti Brothers (fries on the sandwich)

shop

food

activity

Where: Penn Avenue & Smallman Streets

Web: www.neighborsinthestrip.com

Bike the toughest hills of Pittsburgh in the Dirty Dozen annual ride.

This bike ride is a grueling 50 miles but focuses on racing up 13 of the steepest hills in Pittsburgh, and maybe the country. All of the hills exceed a 20 percent grade with one, Canton Avenue, boasting a 37 percent grade. The Dirty Dozen attracts men and women but offers nominal prizes so it is, essentially, a competition based on tenacity and endurance. The race is over 30 years old and rallies enthusiasts each year on the day after Thanksgiving.

activity

Where: Starting point is the Bud Harris
                Cycling Track on Washington Blvd.

Web: http://wesa.fm/post/going-dirty-
                dozen-bike-race-rides-again-
                weekend

Bask in the glow of "light-up night" that ushers the beginning of the Christmas season in the city.

The city tenants leave the lights on to jump start the holiday season. This annual celebration has a tradition of more than 50 years and attracts upwards of 800,000 to the city center. There is plenty to do for all ages on this momentous Friday night after Thanksgiving.

activity   food   music

shop

Where: Throughout downtown Pittsburgh
              city center

Web: http://pittsburgh.about.com/
              cs/downtown/a/light_up_night

Gaze in wonder at the seasonally displayed nativity scene outside of U.S. Steel Tower.

Since 1999, the U.S. Steel Tower plaza has been the site for the larger than life Pittsburgh Creche (nativity scene) that is the world's only authorized replica of the St. Peter's Basilica crèche in Rome, Italy. Visitors can view the Pittsburgh Creche starting on "light up night," the Friday after Thanksgiving. The display is free but public support is needed to continue the tradition.

view

activity

Where: 600 Grant Street
              Pittsburgh, PA 15219
              Donate: The Pittsburgh Creche
              Endowment Fund through The
              Pittsburgh Foundation

Web: www.diopitt.org
              www.pittsburghfoundation.org

Skate at PPG Place for old-fashioned winter fun.

Outdoor skating around a Christmas tree is the attraction each year outside of One PPG Place. Skate rentals are available. When it gets too cold to skate, One PPG Place sells hot cocoa and hosts an international Santa display along with a plentiful exhibition of gingerbread houses. PPG Place covers 5.5 acres in the middle of downtown and is adjacent to Market Square where there are a variety of restaurants for food and relaxation.

activity

food

Where: One PPG Place
                Pittsburgh, PA 15222

Web: www.ppgplace.com

Reconcile with past, present, and future at the annual Christmas Carol show at the Byham Theater.

December in Pittsburgh conjures memories of attending *A Musical Christmas Carol*, sponsored by the Civic Light Opera (CLO). This show has been a Pittsburgh Christmas tradition for more than 20 years and it is based on the 1843 Charles Dickens story entitled, *A Christmas Story*. The classic tale reveals various truths from the past and present with the hopes of changing the foreshadowed future of a miserly businessman named Scrooge.

culture

music

Where:
Heinz Hall
600 Penn Avenue
Pittsburgh, PA 15222
412-456-1390

Web:
http://www.pittsburghclo.org/
shows/view/8/refer:clo-shows

Ring in the New Year with Highmark First Night Festivities.

More than 100 events and activities, both indoor and outdoor, mark this New Years' Eve celebration that consumes much of the Cultural District. The festivities usually begin at 6 p.m. and conclude at midnight. The celebration has been held for more than 20 years and is family-friendly. A moderate "button" fee is required for indoor attractions.

activity   food

Where: Cultural District
                Stanwix Street, Penn & Liberty Avenue
                412-456-6666

Web: www.firstnightpgh.org

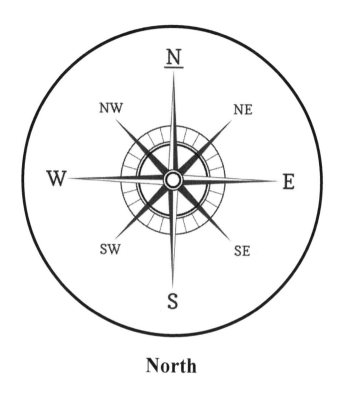

North

· North Side ·Troy Hill

Cool off with an old-fashioned shaved ice from Gus and YiaYia's cart in Riverview Park.

A bright orange cart with and equally bright umbrella has been helping locals beat the heat since 1934. Gus Kalaris started working at his father's cart at age 18 and was still working, at age 80, in 2012. His wife Stella, also called Yia Yia or grandmother in Greek, worked by his side when she was not busy raising their children. Gus and Yia Yia's ice balls are made from chips taken from an ice block as opposed to machine-made ice shavings. Syrups are homemade. There are a multitude of flavors and competitive prices but, more than that, Gus and Yia Yia's is a Pittsburgh summer tradition.

food

Where:	638 West Ohio Street Pittsburgh, PA 15212
Web:	www.pittsburgh.about.com/b/ 2012/06/14/ice-ball-man.htm

Kick back and relax at the ol' ball game—baseball at PNC Park.

PNC Park houses over 38,000 fans and has been the home of the Pittsburgh Pirates since 2001. A variety of ticket prices make the games affordable, depending upon the number of snacks and beverages consumed at in-house restaurants and refreshment stands. With little exception, most seats offer a view of the city that looks over the outfield wall and across the Allegheny River. Some night games include a post-game fireworks display.

activity

Where: PNC Park
               115 Federal Street
               Pittsburgh, PA 15212
               412-321-BUCS

Web: www.pittsburgh.pirates.mlb.com

Tailgate and join the fun -- attend a Pittsburgh Steeler or University of Pittsburgh football game at Heinz Field.

Tailgates and football games are synonymous in Pittsburgh. In fact, some people tailgate despite not having event tickets. Those who are one of the fortunate 65,000 plus to secure a ticket to a game, enjoy an unobstructed view of the city from across the Allegheny River. The Fed Ex Great Hall houses Steeler memorabilia alongside momentos from the University of Pittsburgh Panthers team.

activity

Where: Heinz Field
                100 Art Rooney Avenue
                Pittsburgh, PA 15212
                412-323-1200

Web: www.steelers.com/tickets-and-
                stadium/index.html (stadium info)

Stargaze, explore, and exercise at the Carnegie Science Center and Highmark SportsWorks.

The Science Center has something for all ages and abilities including stargazing the universe in the planetarium, exploring WWII from a submarine, watching a movie in the Omnimax, visiting Pittsburgh via the Miniature Railroad and Village exhibit, and exercising at Highmark SportWorks. Ticket prices vary based on the selected events and shows; Omnimax tickets are often less costly than those at local theaters.

activity

Where   Carnegie Science Center
               One Allegheny Center
               Pittsburgh, PA 15212
               412-237-3400

Web: www.carnegiesciencecenter.org

Run, jog, or walk the annual Turkey Trot on Thanksgiving.

The PNC YMCA Turkey Trot offers a way to work off pounds before the feast. The annual event is more than 23 years old and is held on Thanksgiving morning. Starting at PNC Park, participants can run or walk a 5k or a 1 mile route. There is a warm and festive atmosphere among the fit, and not-so-fit, on this chilly November morning.

activity

Where: 115 Federal Street
            Pittsburgh, PA 15212

Web: www.ymcaofpittsburgh.org

Play at the Pittsburgh Children's Museum.

Capturing an elusive shadow, walking across a tilted floor, creating interesting puppet shows, exploring test driving equipment, playing in a large doll house, and engaging in creative activities for tots are a few examples of Children's Museum exhibits. Of course, the fun is always changing so it is best to look at the website for current details.

activity

Where: Pittsburgh Children's Museum
10 Children's Way
Allegheny Square
Pittsburgh, PA 15212

Web: www.pittsburghkids.com

Listen to the birds chirp at the National Aviary.

Every continent except Antarctica is represented at the Aviary. Exhibits are designed for free-flight and mixed species in order to replicate a natural habitat and there are more than 500 birds and 150 species represented. The National Aviary is involved in education, conservation, and camping events for all ages. Based on the age of the visitor, close encounters and experiences are available such as: trainer for a day or trekking with the flamingos.

activity

Where: National Aviary
                 700 Arch Street
                 Pittsburgh, PA 15212
                 412-323-7235

Web: www.aviary.org

Investigate the origins of the universe at the Allegheny Observatory.

The Allegheny Observatory is an astronomical research institution that is operated by the University of Pittsburgh Department of Physics & Astronomy. This fact may not garner attention but free weekly tours and monthly lectures do. Lecture topics focus on exploding stars, universe simulation, dark matter, and mysteries of the universe. Thursday night tours are available from April through August and Friday night tours extend to November 1st. Reservations are required. See the website for details.

view

activity

Where: Allegheny Observatory
                159 Riverview Avenue
                Pittsburgh, PA 15214
                412-321-2400

Web: www.pitt.edu/~aobsvtry/tours

Relish the glory and grandeur of an earlier time on a Christmas tour of the Mexican War streets.

The Mexican War Streets were designed following the Mexican-American War. Despite the development of local life, in what was then considered Allegheny City, the 1920s migration to the suburbs started a trend that left the area as a target for demolition by the 1960s. Thanks to the efforts of the Pittsburgh History and Landmarks Foundation and the Mexican War Streets Society, the area experienced a significant resurgence. Holiday tours of selected homes give visitors a glimpse of the grandeur.

activity

Where: Mexican War Streets Society
                P.O. Box 6588
                Pittsburgh, PA 15212

Web: www.mexicanwarstreets.org

Savor the flavor of a pastrami sandwich, or other specialties, at Max's Allegheny Tavern on Suisman Street.

This Tavern dates back to the early 1900s when the area was developed by English, Scottish, Irish, and German settlers. Once a hotel and Prohibition-era speakeasy, this local tavern in what was commonly known as Dutchtown, now specializes in German food and brew as evidenced in the flag colors that decorate the website. The reuben sandwich and the kase spatzles are favorites but the authentic atmosphere, menu variety, and modern ratskeller, complete the experience.

food

Where: Max's Allegheny Tavern
                537 Suismon Street
                Pittsburgh, PA 15212
                412-231-1899

Web: www.maxsalleghenytavern.com

Take in the Andy Warhol museum for an avant garde artist's view of life.

Cultural icon Andy Warhol was born in Pittsburgh and his art is known around the world. The Pittsburgh-based Andy Warhol Museum houses seven floors of Warhol's works, tracing his experimentation with mediums and subject matter, from the 1940s to the 1980s. The Warhol is one of four museums supported by the Carnegie Museums of Pittsburgh. A valid ID from selected universities will guarantee free access for students.

culture

activity

Where: The Andy Warhol Museum
117 Sandusky Street
Pittsburgh, PA 15212
412-237-8300

Web: www.warhol.org

Hike or drive down Rialto Street that extends from Troy Hill to Route 28—summer months only.

Rialto Street, a.k.a., "pig hill," is a destination to behold in the Troy Hill neighborhood. The street was used to drive pigs toward Herr's Island (today known as Washington's Landing) but today it offers mere convenience to other destinations for local residents. The street is 20 feet wide and has a 24% grade so it often stops the best of cyclists and certainly slows hikers and walkers too. For the less adventuresome, a look down Rialto Street may be enough.

activity

Where: Rialto Street
                  Pittsburgh, PA 15212

Web: www.troyhillpittsburgh.com

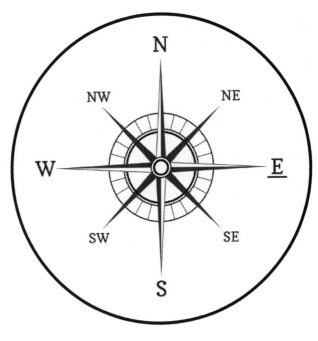

East

·Oakland · Squirrel Hill ·Shadyside
·East Liberty ·Point Breeze
·Lawrenceville·Highland Park

Delight in "Dippy" the dinosaur and his friends at the Carnegie Museum of Natural History.

Dippy, a life-sized replica of the museum's first dinosaur discovery, greets Oakland visitors on Forbes Avenue. Often adorned in a hat and scarf, Dippy has a dedicated online museum scrapbook and is the public face for his more imposing friends who reside inside. Other permanent exhibits focus on geological, anthropological, wild life, and botanical subjects. "Hands on" activities for children happen at Discovery Basecamp and the Bonehunters' Quarry.

culture   activity

Where: Carnegie Museum of Natural History - 4400 Forbes Avenue Pittsburgh, PA 15213 412-622-3131

Web: www.carnegiemnh.org

Appreciate the talent and variety of artwork at the Carnegie Museum of Art (CMOA) -- sculpture, print, painting, drawing, architectural, decorative, photographs, digital, or film.

The CMOA houses a permanent collection of more than 35,000 objects and a serves as a home to the *Carnegie International,* the "oldest exhibition of international contemporary art in North America" (CMOA website, 2014). In addition to permanent and visiting exhibitions, the CMOA offers classes, lectures, and publications. A valid ID from selected universities will guarantee free access for students.

culture   activity

Where: Carnegie Museum of Art
                4400 Forbes Avenue (at Craig)
                Pittsburgh, PA 15213
                412-622-3131

Web: www.cmoa.org/visit/

Linger in the stacks of the formidable Carnegie Library of Pittsburgh.

The Carnegie Library of Pittsburgh (CLP) was founded in 1895 by steel magnate Andrew Carnegie and is situated amidst the surrounding pillars of academia at the University of Pittsburgh and Carnegie Mellon University.   Each year, the CLP offers a substantial amount of community programming, attracts more than 2.2 million visitors, and loans more than 3.5 million items.

culture   activity

Where: Carnegie Library of Pittsburgh
                4400 Forbes Avenue
                Pittsburgh, PA 15213
                412-622-3114

Web: carnegielibrary.org

Scale the heights of the Cathedral of Learning (with the help of an elevator).

The Cathedral of Learning is Pittsburgh's Eiffel Tower. This Gothic cathedral soars 42 floors, or 535 feet, above the Oakland landscape and is visible from many city vantage points. Those who navigate the elevators to floor 36 are offered a panorama of city views. Floors 37- 42 are reserved for occupants only.

For those who prefer to remain closer to the ground, the first and third floors house Nationality Rooms that offer a glimpse of the culture and ethnicities that belonged to early Allegheny County settlers. The rooms are a popular destination and attract more than 30,000 visitors each year with guided tours available for groups of 10 or more and audio guides available for smaller groups. Explanatory plaques describe the interiors for those who prefer to wander independently. If touring is not of interest, the common study area on the first floor transports visitors to scenes from a *Harry Potter* film.

culture

activity

Additional ground-based places of interest, adjacent to the Cathedral, are the Stephen Foster Memorial and the nondenominational, 75 year-old Heinz Memorial Chapel. Respective websites offer details.

Where: Between Forbes and Fifth Avenues
                4200 Fifth Avenue
                Pittsburgh, PA 15260
                412-624-4141

Web: Cathedral of Learning
                www.tour.pitt.edu

                Stephen Foster Memorial
                www.pitt.edu~amerimus/Museum
                www.play.pitt.edu

                Heinz Chapel
                www.heinzchapel.pittedu

Expand existing horizons or find a religious niche with a visit to St. Paul's Cathedral, Rodef Shalom, the Islamic Center of Pittsburgh, or the Three Rivers Dharma Center.

Pittsburgh exhibits tolerance and acceptance of diverse religious practices. The destinations mentioned are only a few examples of the diversity of faith systems in practice in Pittsburgh. Leaders of each facility are welcoming to guests as well as faithful followers. If private discussions or tours are of interest, arrangements can be made prior to a visit. Website sections for frequently asked questions offer additional information about practices, expectations, and accessibility.

culture

activity

Where / Web: Multiple locations in Oakland
-North Dithridge
-Fifth Avenue
-Bigelow Boulevard
-South Craig Street

St. Paul's Cathedral (Roman Catholic – Christian)
108 North Dithridge Street
Pittsburgh, PA 15213-2608
412-621-4951
www.stpaulpgh.org

Rodef Shalom (Reform Judaism)
4905 Fifth Avenue
Pittsburgh, PA 15213
412-621-6566
www.rodefshalom.org

Islamic Center of Pittsburgh (Muslim)
4100 Bigelow Boulevard
Pittsburgh, PA 15213
412-682-5555
www.icp-pgh.org

Three Rivers Dharma Center (Tibetan Buddhism)
201 S. Craig Street (Enter on Henry Street)
Pittsburgh, PA 15213
www.threeriversdharma.org

Lunch at the "O," otherwise known as The Original Hot Dog Shop.

The "O" is iconic lunch and snack stop for university students, residents, and anyone passing by this Oakland institution. Hot dogs and fries are the featured fare – hot dog topping choices and cheese on the fries make the meal. The "O" is a family run business that started during the Pittsburgh Pirates championship season of 1960 and it has sustained its' status as an Oakland "go to" place for dining in or take out.

food

Where: The Original Hot Dog Shop
            Corner - Forbes Ave. & Atwood St.
            3901 Forbes Avenue
            Pittsburgh, PA 15213
            412-621-7388

Web: www.theoriginalhotdogshop.com

Climb "Cardiac Hill" (Lothrop Street) to Peterson Event Center.

Cardiac Hill used to lead students and visitors to Saturday football games at Pitt Stadium with convenient stops at local hospitals for those faint of heart on the way up. Nowadays, those climbing the hill are likely on the way to the University of Pittsburgh Peterson Event Center. The Center hosts University of Pittsburgh basketball games, fitness facilities, and commencement exercises in addition to serving as a venue for smaller concerts. This hill has its own website that is maintained by students and Pitt alumni.

activity

Where: Fifth and Lothrop Streets
Pittsburgh, PA 15213

Web: www.cardiachill.com
www.petersoneventscenter.com

Witness Pittsburgh Pirate baseball history at the 1960 home run wall of Bill Mazeroski.

The University of Pittsburgh Katz School of Business and Posvar Hall rest on what was Forbes Field, former home to the Pittsburgh Pirates and Steelers and the University of Pittsburgh football team (pre-Pitt Stadium and Heinz Field). Home plate is located inside Posvar Hall. The Forbes Field centerfield wall is replicated near Katz (Mervis Hall) and marks the site where Pirate second baseman, Bill Mazeroski, hit a homerun to win the 1960 World Series.

view

Where: Roberto Clemente Drive
Pittsburgh, PA 15260
(Between Schenley & S. Bouquet)

Web: www.clpgh.org/exhibit/
neighborhoods/oakland/
oak_n713.html

**Stop and smell the flowers at Phipps Conservatory –
especially vibrant to welcome the winter and spring
seasons.**

Phipps Conservatory and Botanical Gardens is a Victorian-era
greenhouse that offers a year-round destination for those who
appreciate being in nature. Special exhibits for winter and
spring holidays offer prime-time views to visitors but the
foliage and warmer climate of the conservatory is welcoming
during any inclement Pittsburgh day.

view

activity

Where: Phipps Conservatory
                One Schenley Park
                Pittsburgh, PA 15213
                412-622-6914

Web: www.phippsconservatory.org

Sled or sun on Flagstaff Hill.

Carnegie Mellon University and University of Pittsburgh students converge on Flagstaff Hill. The sloped green lawn sits across the street from Phipps Conservatory and offers a summer gathering place for movie watching, sun-seeking, kite flying, and studying. The Hill has also been a source of sled riding or modified snowboarding during the winter months.

activity

Where: Green space across from
                One Schenley Drive
                Pittsburgh, PA   15213

Web: www.pittsburghparks.org/park

Stroll, bike, jog, or skate in Schenley Park.

Schenley Park offers hiking, jogging, and biking, in addition to seasonal skating and swimming. The park has 456 acres of trails, woods, and attractions. The Schenley Oval offers a dedicated space for exercise with a running track, a soccer field, and an ice skating rink. Anderson Park features castle and dinosaur climbing and slides and is across the bridge from Phipps Conservatory. Refreshments are sold at the restored, 100 year-old, Schenley Park Café and Visitor Center. A trail map is posted outside the Café.

activity

Where: Multiple entrance points
              -Schenley Drive near Phipps
              -Greenfield Road at Hobart Street
              -Greenfield Road at Bartlett Street

Web: www.pittsburghparks.org/park

Stop to play, picnic, exercise, or relax, at other Pittsburgh "Citiparks."

Citiparks provide green space to residents and visitors. Frick Park features walking trails, playgrounds, tennis courts, and baseball fields on 644 acres. Highland Park offers a tree covered "super" playground and walking paths on 500 acres near a reservoir. Mellon Park Tennis Center, a.k.a. the "bubble," allows for year-round play. The Oliver Bath House offers season swimming passes to city residents for fall, winter, and spring use. Outdoor summer pools are available to city residents.

activity

Where: Multiple entrance points

Web: www.pittsburghparks.org/park
                www.pittsburghpa.gov/citiparks/

Participate in civic events, enjoy concerts, and attend lectures at the Jewish Community Center.

The Jewish Community Center (JCC) is an expansive resource and a central gathering space for the Squirrel Hill community. The JCC focuses on enduring values in a changing world as exemplified through varied programming that includes travel opportunities, cultural events, childcare, and athletics. Discounts for students and monthly payment plans are available.

activity   culture

Where: Jewish Community Center
                5738 Forbes Avenue
                Pittsburgh, PA 15217
                412-521-8010

Web: www.jccpgh.org

Enjoy dining al fresco, shopping for Fair Trade specialties, or local urban life in Squirrel Hill.

The Squirrel Hill community is a lively urban setting with easy access to Oakland. This section of the city is a blend of residential and institutional development that is focused on families and young professionals. There is a Carnegie Library branch in addition to a number of restaurants, shops, educational facilities, and religious spaces.

activity   food   shop

Where: Business -
                Squirrel Hill Urban Coalition
                5604 Solway Street
                Pittsburgh, PA 15217

Web: www.shuc.org

Saunter through the Shadyside Arts Festival.

The Annual Art Festival on Walnut Street is comprised of boutique vendors and has been supported by local retailers and community residents for more than 16 years. The festival features artists, craftsman, jewelers, photographers, and others who offer sale items for a variety of budgets. There are also a number of food establishments and booths to keep shoppers refreshed.

culture   shop   food

Where: Patrons-739 Bellfonte St.
                Pittsburgh, PA 15232

                Exhibitors-
                Info@ArtFestival.com
                561-746-6615

Web: www.artfestival.com

Purchase unique gifts for friends and family at Kards Unlimited.

Kards Unlimited offers a Hallmark antithesis with an eclectic array of gifts, cards, books, and novelty items such as politically charged greeting cards, colorful "nag notes," novelty ice cubes, intriguing reading material, retro toys, novelty shot glasses, Harry Potter regalia, and explicitly designed T-shirts. More common items include cookbooks, hand lotions, calendars, and greeting cards.

shop

Where: Kards Unlimited
                5522 Walnut Street
                Pittsburgh, PA 15232
                412-622-0500

Web: http://kardsunlimited.com/about/

Savor the flavor and chatter of local coffee shops - Crazy Mocha and The Coffee Tree Roasters.

Crazy Mocha and The Coffee Tree Roasters are native to Pittsburgh and share a lot in common. Both focus on neighborhoods, comfort, and coffee. Patrons stop to chat with friends, to study, or to conduct business meetings. Both offer free Wi-Fi and both offer a variety of scrumptious snacks; notable are Crazy Mocha's trail mixes or iced biscotti and The Coffee Tree Roasters Coconut Caramels or flavored straws.

food

activity

Where: Various-

                Crazy Mocha – 30 locations
                The Coffee Tree – 6 locations

Web: www.crazymocha.com
                www.coffeetree.com/

Peruse the sweet treats of Prantl's Bakery.

Prantl's Bakery started more than 40 years ago and has continued to thrive, despite competition from local grocery stores and independent bakeries, and despite the retirement of founders Henry and Jane Prantl. The two locations, Market Square and Shadyside, offer seasonal specialties, dinner desserts, and one-of-a-kind creations for one-of-a-kind events.

food

Where: Prantl's Bakery
                5525 Walnut Street
                Shadyside, PA 15232
                412-621-2092
                info@prantlsbakery.com

Web: infoms@prantlsbakery.com

Stroll the streets of Shadyside Business District.

Shadyside offers shopping, pampering, restaurants, cafes, and Warm Weather Walks for patrons in the neighborhood or those traveling from nearby suburbs. There are over 80 independent and national shops situated in Shadyside; retailers sell everything from athletic apparel to furniture to kids toys. Special events and festivals give added incentive to visitors who must navigate parking and driving on the narrow streets of Shadyside.

shop   food   activity

Where: Shadyside Chamber of Commerce
                5501 Walnut Street – Suite 201
                Pittsburgh, PA 15232
                412-682-1298

Web: www.thinkshadyside.com

Express yourself at the Pittsburgh Center for the Arts (PCA) and the Pittsburgh Filmmakers (PF).

The PCA and PF give artists and want-to-be artists a place to learn, exchange, and create. Available classes include: painting, sculpting, drawing, printing, media, photography, and filmmaking. Workshops are offered to people of all ages, talents, and interests.

activity

Where: Pittsburgh Center for the Arts
           1047 Shady Avenue (at Fifth Ave.)
           Pittsburgh, PA 15232
           412-361-0873

           Pittsburgh Filmmakers
           477 Melwood Avenue
           Pittsburgh, PA 15213
           412-681-5449

Web: pittsburgharts.org/

Discover the freshest organics at the East End Food Co-op (EEFC) or Whole Foods Market.

Fresh organics, seasonal produce, special events, minimal processing, and knowledgeable staff, are common denominators of these two East End food purveyors. Both stores opened in the 1980s; the Food Co-op is locally owned and operated. Whole Foods is a national chain but part of the Conscious Capitalist movement.

shop

Where: East End Food Coop
                7516 Meade Street
                Pittsburgh, PA 15208
                412-242-3598

                Whole Foods Market
                5880 Centre Avenue
                Pittsburgh, PA 15206
                412-441-7960

Web: www.eastendfood.coop/co-op
                www.wholefoodsmarket.com

Enter the Industrial Age for the afternoon and visit the Frick Art & Historical Center.

Pittsburgh is often associated with the steel industry. The fuel for the steel mills, in the form of coke, was created by industrialist Henry Clay Frick. Frick and his growing family lived in Pittsburgh during the late 1800s and then maintained connections to the city after moving to New York City in 1905. The Frick Art Museum opened in 1970, the family residence (Clayton) was restored and opened in 1990, the Café opened in 1994, and the Car and Carriage Museum opened in 1997.

culture   activity

Where: Frick Art & Historical Center
                7227 Reynolds Street
                Pittsburgh, PA 15208
                412-371-0600

Web: www.thefrickpittsburgh.org

Indulge in all things French during lunch or dinner at Paris 66, Pittsburgh's French bistro in the East End.

Pittsburgh's Best French Restaurant transports visitors; many of the wait staff speak French, the décor is from the bistros of Paris, and the food is authentic French fare. The menu includes lunch, dinner, special events, and Parisian Ladurée-style pastries. The pastries, otherwise known as exquisite confections, are created by Chef Piquard and also sold at the Gaby and Jules store in Squirrel Hill.

food   culture

Where: Paris 66
            6018 Penn Circle South
            Pittsburgh, PA 15206
            412-404-8166

Web: www.paris66bistro.com
            www.gabyetjules.com

Walk on the wild side at the Pittsburgh Zoo and Aquarium.

This is one of six major zoo and aquarium facilities in the country and it is situated on 77 acres. The animals reside in replicas of natural surroundings, but all are wild, so caution should be exercised. For younger visitors, the Kids Kingdom offers a place to play and safely interact with selected species and with the assistance of zoo staff. The Zoo and Aquarium are open 365 days a year with the exception of Thanksgiving, Christmas, and New Years Day.

activity

Where: Pittsburgh Zoo and Aquarium
                7340 Butler Street
                Pittsburgh, PA 15206
                412-665-3640

Web: www.pittsburghzoo.org

Browse, dine, gallery hop, or stroll through the neighborhood streets of Lawrenceville.

Lawrenceville is a revitalized section of the city and is located less than three miles from downtown. Artists arrived first to occupy the work and gallery space. Craftspeople, designers, and residents followed. This affordable community is in transition but offers convenience and an eclectic array of new storefronts to frequent.

activity   shop   food

Where: The Lawrenceville Corporation
                c/o The Ice House Studios
                100 43rd Street
                Pittsburgh, PA 15201

Web: www.lvpgh.com

Look and listen for the spirits in the Allegheny or Homewood Cemeteries.

The cemeteries serve as the final resting place for many prestigious and well-known Pittsburgh families. Both were opened in the 1800s, both include substantial acreage, and both offer nature and serenity to visitors.

activity

Where: Allegheny – 4734 Butler St.
                Pittsburgh, PA 15201
                412-682-1624

                Homewood – 1599 S. Dallas Ave.
                Pittsburgh, PA 15217
                412- 421-1822

Web: www.alleghenycemetery.com
                www.thehomewoodcemetery.com

Discover a new path to enlightenment at the Church Brew Works.

The Church Brew Works is located on the site of a former Roman Catholic Church that was built in 1902 and was decommissioned in 1993. The former alter features brewing equipment, but that is only one of the novelties that attract patrons.

food

activity

Where: Church Brew Works
3525 Liberty Avenue
Pittsburgh, PA 15201
412-688-8200

Web: www.churchbrew.com/

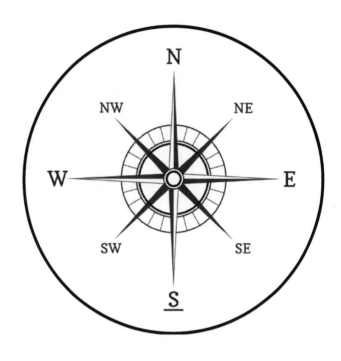

South

·Station Square ·South Side

Shop, eat, tour, or wander through the dining and entertainment establishments in Station Square.

Entertainment options are plentiful at Station Square. Lunch or dinner at the Hard Rock Café, spray from the Fountain at Bessemer Court, sporting events and concerts at Highmark Stadium, horse-drawn carriage rides, boat cruises on the Gateway Clipper fleet, or drinks at the Sheraton River Room give visitors a multitude of choices for entertainment.

activity   food   shop

Where: Station Square
                125 West Station Square Drive
                Pittsburgh, PA 15219
                412-261-2811

Web: www.stationsquare.com

Ride the Monongahela or Duquesne inclines from Station Square to Mt. Washington for a city view.

The inclines are over 130 years old, have 30+ degree grades, are actively used for commuters and visitors, and are among a few remaining in the country. The inclines have stations atop Mt. Washington and near Station Square. Both inclines operate 365 days a year for 17+ hours a day. Exact change is needed. See the websites for details.

activity

view

Where/Web: Monongahela Incline
              East Carson Street- Pgh., PA 15211
              412-361-0873
              www.portauthority.org/paac

              The Duquesne Incline
              West Carson Street-Pgh., PA 15219
              412-381-1665
              www.duquesneincline.org

Indulge in savory selections from the Grand Concourse restaurant located in Station Square.

The Grand Concourse is located in the former Pittsburgh and Lake Erie Station that was built near the turn of the 20th century. The stained glass cathedral roof houses a majestic facility that still features some of the original materials such as brass, marble, and mahogany. The menu is varied and prepared to order. Piano music often accompanies weekend meals. The adjoining Gandy Dancer Saloon provides a pre-meal or athletic game day refreshment stop.

food

Where: Grand Concourse
            125 West Station Square Drive
            Pittsburgh, PA 15219
            412-261-1717

Web: www.muer.com/grand-concourse/

Cruise on a game day riverboat shuttle or for relaxation with the Gateway Clipper Fleet.

Station Square is the launch point for shuttle service to Pirate baseball games at PNC Park or Steeler/Pitt football games at Heinz Field. Shuttle service is one of many options available from the Gateway Clipper Fleet. Since 1958, other offerings have included cruises for dinner, education, entertainment, weddings, and school events. The riverboat fleet consists of six vessels with capacities from 600 to 1,000 passengers.

activity

view

food

Where: Gateway Clipper Fleet
              350 West Station Square Drive
              Pittsburgh, PA 15219
              412-355-7980

Web: www.gatewayclipper.com

Enjoy budget beverages (in moderation) at Jack's.

Moving up the Allegheny River to South Side introduces customers to a new set of daytime or evening entertainment options at places such as Jack's. Jack's is a popular Pittsburgh stop that offers alcohol specials and entertainment from 7 a.m. until 2 a.m. Monday through Saturday and Sundays from 9 a.m. until 2 a.m. The South Side location makes it easily accessible to local residents and college students. Light fare and snacks are also served.

food

Where: Jack's Bar
                1117 East Carson Street
                Pittsburgh, PA 15203
                412-431-6344

Web: http://www.jacksbarpittsburgh.com/

Shop, stroll, and dine in the South Side.

The South Side is a package of residential and commercial, old and new, eclectic and mainstream. The eclectic boutiques and local specialty stores are generally found between 10th and 18th streets. The mainstream chains and larger restaurants are typically found between 24th and 28th streets. The South Side's proximity to local universities results in the area becoming a hub of evening activity.

activity

shop

food

Where: South Side Chamber of Commerce
1100 East Carson Street
Pittsburgh, PA 15203
412-431-3360

Web: www.southsidechamber.org

Celebrate cultural diversity in the South Side.

There are many ethnic eateries in the Pittsburgh's South Side. German food at the Hofbräuhaus, Irish at the Claddagh Irish Pub, Italian at Dish Osteria, Spanish at Mallorca, and Japanese at Nakama Japanese Steakhouse are just a few names that come to mind. Some are located along Carson Street but the South Side Chamber of Commerce has more details on each of these establishments. See the website for details and locations.

food

Where: Various locations
              South Side Chamber of Commerce
              1100 East Carson Street
              Pittsburgh, PA 15203
              412-431-3360

Web: www.southsidechamber.org/
              business_directory/

Bike the Three Rivers Heritage Trail path in and around the city to South Side.

There are many access points to the 22 miles of bike and pedestrian trails that are adjacent to Pittsburgh's Allegheny, Monongahela, and Ohio rivers. The parking facilities near the "Hot Metal Bridge" offer an easy point of entry to this network that extends from the South Side, to downtown, to the North Shore and beyond.

activity

Where: Friends of the Riverfront, Inc.
                33 Terminal Way – Suite 333B
                Pittsburgh, PA 15219
                412-488-0212

Web: www.friendsoftheriverfront.org

Gobble a cool cone from Page's ice cream stand; before or after work or sometime in between.

Homemade ice cream has been the primary pleasure for over 60 years. The cones and sundaes are worth waiting in a line that sometimes snakes its way around the side of the building. Local specialties, such as the South Side milk shake or a Yinzer Sunday are served alongside standard ice cream flavors and toppings, arctic swirls, and local baked goods.

food

Where: Page Dairy Mart
                4600 East Carson Street
                Pittsburgh, PA 15210
                Beneath the railway trestle-
                Becks Run Rd. and East Carson St.
                412-431-0600

Web: www.pagedairymart.net

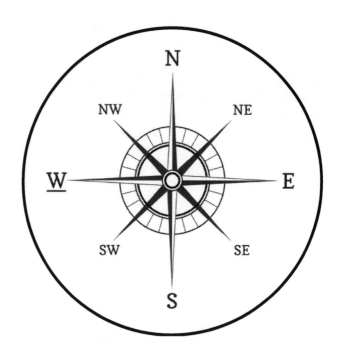

West

· West End

Sneak up to the West End Overlook for a great view of the city.

Tucked into the hills above Elliott and the West End is the Overlook. This green space offers a unique view of the city, free movies during the summer, and an unparalleled vantage point for the Fourth of July fireworks. In addition, the Elliott Community Group partnered with local government and Comcast internet to offer free Wi-Fi access at the "Overlook." See the website for log on details.

view

Where: Access by 920 Rue Grande Vue St.
                Access by 601 Fairview Avenue
                Pittsburgh, PA 15220

Web: www.elliottcg.org
                www.pittsburghpa.gov/citiparks

Investigate the potential of Pittsburgh's West End Village.

Located 5 minutes from downtown and 20 minutes from the airport, this location is one to consider for young professionals. West End Village is in a state of renewal.   In recent years, with the help of the West Pittsburgh Partnership for Regional Development (WPP), West End has added more than 35 businesses and attracted investment of more than $11 million dollars. This neighborhood is worth a look.

activity

Where: West Pittsburgh Partnership
                438 South Main Street
                Pittsburgh, PA 15220
                412-922-2740

Web: www.west-end-village.com

city limits

Drive across city lines to Homestead and slip down the water slides at Sandcastle Water Park.

Sandcastle offers a refreshing alternative to help visitors beat the heat. There is a wave pool and a lazy river for those who prefer to lounge around. For the rest of the crowd, there are a variety of water slides, most of which require riders to sit on an inflatable inner tube and enjoy a rapid ride. The plunging "lightning *express*" is a bit more daring and requires riders to free-fall down a body chute. Details and prices are available on the website.

activity

Where: Sandcastle Water Park
                1000 Sandcastle Drive
                Pittsburgh, PA 15120
                412-462-6666

Web: www.sandcastlewaterpark.com

Eat, shop, or walk through the shops and restaurants at the Waterfront complex.

The Waterfront opened in 1999 on the site of the former U.S. Steel Homestead Works. The Homestead Works closed in 1987 but the stacks remain as a testament to the thousands of workers who spent a lifetime helping to build the U.S. steel industry. The shopping area is located in West Homestead, Homestead, and Munhall and offers a variety of restaurants, hotels, shops, and entertainment venues.

shop

food

activity

Where: The Waterfront
                149 W. Bridge Street
                Homestead, PA 15120
                412-476-8889

Web: www.waterfrontpgh.com

Seek the thrills at Kennywood Amusement Park in West Mifflin.

This park offers thrills for riders of all ages and fear factors. There are wooden roller coasters, water rides, steel coasters, and everything in between, including rocking, spinning, and circling 360 degrees. Everyone has favorites including older rides such as the Jack Rabbit, Racer, and Thunderbolt; newer rides such as the Black Widow or Aero 360; or others such as the Pirate and Phantom's Revenge. Detailed descriptions are shown on the website.

activity

Where: Kennywood Amusement Park
           4800 Kennywood Boulevard
           West Mifflin, PA 15122
           412-461-0500

Web: www.kennywood.com

Dip, slide, or jump into the cool waters of Dormont Pool.

Dormont Pool provides cool refreshment to residents and non-residents. The Olympic-sized pool opened in the 1920s and experienced a renewal in 2006. At that time, the Friends of Dormont Pool rallied resources, residents, and pool patrons, to fund significant repair costs. Kids enjoy the slide and mushroom-styled fountain. Adults enjoy the clean surroundings, a plentiful snack bar, and easy pool access from various entry points. Cabanas are available for private rental.

activity

Where: Dormont Pool
                1801 Dormont Avenue
                Pittsburgh, PA 15216
                412-341-7210

Web: www.boro.dormont.pa.us/

Stroll, dine, drink, and shop in the many storefronts of Mt. Lebanon.

Mount Lebanon is a suburb located south of the city that supports several business districts, each of which features a variety of restaurants and retail establishments. This suburb is known for blending retail with residential and includes neighborhood schools, parks, and ample athletic facilities. Il Pizzaiolo and Bistro 19 lure the lunch and dinner crowds but there are numerous dining, shopping, and socializing options for any rendezvous.

shop

food

activity

Where:　　　　Mount Lebanon Municipal Offices
　　　　　　　710 Washington Road
　　　　　　　Pittsburgh, PA 15228-2018
　　　　　　　412-343-3400

Web:　　　　　www.mtlebanon.org

Embrace a haunted Halloween tradition of thrills and chills.

"Phantom Fright Nights," the Scarehouse, Hundred Acres Manor, and Terror Town are several places for thrills and chills during the Halloween season in Pittsburgh. Less intense are Pittsburgh ZooBoo nights and Spooky Science sleepovers. Most start at the beginning of October and range in price and audience.

activity

Where: Phantom Fright Night-Kennywood
                       Scarehouse – Locust St. in Etna
                       Hundred Acres at Bethel Park, PA
                       Terror Town – Strip District

Web: www.phantomfrightnights.com
                       www.scarehouse.com
                       www.hundredacresmanor.com
                       www.terrortownpgh.com

Shop until you drop at a variety of indoor and outdoor malls -- South Hills Village, Ross Park Mall, Robinson Town Center, the Mall at Robinson, and The Pointe.

South Hills Village is located south of the city and serves as a hub for local shoppers with 130 specialty stores. Nearby restaurants, theaters, and an adjacent Barnes and Noble add entertainment options.

Ross Park Mall is located north of the city and features 170 retailers. Most notable names include department stores such as Macy's, J.C. Penney, Sears, and Nordstrum as well as specialty stores such as Armani, Kate Spade, Tiffany's, Louis Vuitton, Burberry, Juicy Couture, and Michael Kors.

.

Robinson Town Center is west of the city and features an outdoor shopping space with more than 50 shops and restaurants near the Mall at Robinson. The Mall is adjacent to Robinson Town Center and is an indoor facility with over 120 stores and kiosks to satisfy shoppers. The Pointe, located in North Fayette, is within eyesight from both and is accessible via access road from the Mall or from the Parkway West (I-376). All shopping venues are only 7 miles from the airport.

shop   activity   food

Where/Web: Multiple locations

South Hills Village
301 S. Hills Village
Bethel Park, PA 15241-1400
412-831-8652
www.simon.com

Ross Park Mall
1000 Ross Park Mall Drive
Pittsburgh, PA 15237-3875
412-369-4401
www.simon.com

Robinson Town Center
Park manor Boulevard
Pittsburgh, PA 15205
www.robinsontowncentre.com
www.shoprobinsonmall.com

The Mall at Robinson
100 Robinson Centre Drive
Pittsburgh, PA 15205
http://www.shoprobinsonmall.com/directions

The Pointe at North Fayette
Summit Park Drive
North Fayette Township, PA 15275

Step back in time and stroll the streets in Sewickley.

Sewickley Borough, also known as "The Village," is located west of the city. The Village is quaint and offers community resources within a one square mile business district. Shops, restaurants, cafes, give this place a real sense of community. Favorites include retro sweets and soda from Village Candy, lunch or dinner and truffle fries at the Sewickley Café, artistic indulgence at the Clay Café, and kid's stuff at Fun-Buy-the-Pound.

food

shop

activity

Where: Sewickley Borough
            601 Thorn Street
            Sewickley, PA 15143
            412-741-4015

Web: www.sewickleyborough.org

Indulge in the chocolate and ice cream at Sarris Candies in Canonsburg.

The creamy milk chocolate of Sarris Candies was first served more than 50 years ago and now appears in more than 800 retail outlets. The store occupies an entire block and, in addition to chocolate, sells homemade ice cream with tasty toppings. Melted caramel and a milk chocolate hard cap are a dynamic combination. Most impressive is the chocolate castle which stands 12 feet tall and weighs 2,600 pounds.

food

shop

Where: Sarris Candies
            511 Adams Avenue
            Canonsburg, PA
            724-745-4042

Web: www.sarriscandies.com

Dance to the music at outdoor concert venues: First Niagara Pavilion, Stage AE, Hartwood Acres, and Highmark Stadium.

First Niagara Pavilion provides amphitheater concert space for 23,000 fans and is located just 25 miles west of the city.

Stage AE offers a reversible stage that can accommodate indoor or outdoor concerts. The facility size varies depending on the size of the crowd; maximum size is 2,400 seats.

Hartwood Acres is located on 629 acres northeast of Pittsburgh. Hartwood features tours of the 16th century mansion, tea parties, concerts, and more.

Highmark Stadium is home to the Pittsburgh Riverhounds Professional Soccer Club. Stadium seating is 3,500 for games but expands to nearly 10,000 for concerts.

music

activity

Where/Web: Multiple locations

First Niagara
665 Route 18
Burgettstown, PA 15021
724-947-7400
www.ticketmaster.com
www.firstniagarapavilion.net

Stage AE
400 N. Shore Drive
Pittsburgh, PA 15212
412-229-5483
www.ticketmaster.com

Hartwood Acres
200 Hartwood Acres
Pittsburgh, PA 15238
www.alleghenycounty.us./parks
412-767-9200

Highmark Stadium
510 W.Station Square Drive
Pittsburgh, PA 15219
www.highmarkstadium.com
412-224-4900

Ski at local resorts such as Boyce Park, Seven Springs, or Hidden Valley.

Snow is not always plentiful but if nature does not provide it, these resorts make it themselves. Boyce is about 30 minutes from the city and Hidden Valley and Seven Springs are double that time; all are great outdoor spaces.

Boyce Park is an Allegheny County Park and offers gentle slopes for new skiers and snowboarders, as well as tubing for non-skiers. The location is affordable for families and a convenient place for to practice for those with downhill experience.

Hidden Valley and Seven Springs are year-round playgrounds but are known predominantly as ski resorts. Hidden Valley has 31 slopes and Seven Springs has 33 and both offer 11 lifts. Lodging, rentals, food, drink, spa, and wedding services are available year-round. Summer activities include: golf, mountain biking, swimming, and hiking.

activity

view

Where/Web: Multiple locations

Boyce Park
675 Old Frankstown Road
Pittsburgh, PA 15239
www.alleghenycounty.us
724-733-4656

Hidden Valley Resort
One Craighead Drive
Hidden Valley, PA 15502
814-443-8000
www.hiddenvalleyresort.com

Seven Springs Mountain Resort
777 Waterwheel Drive
Seven Springs, PA 15622
800-452-2223
www.7springs.com

Wander through the county parks.

Walking, jogging, biking, boating, ice skating, theater going, and pony riding, add to the concerts, BMX track, dog park, tennis courts, and other amenities available in North and South Park. All offer outdoor green space and a variety of other entertainment for the enjoyment of visitors including a summer triathlon for kids. See the website for additional parks and information.

activity

Where: North – 3,075 acres
                 Pearce Mill Road
                 Allison Park, PA 15101
                 724-935-1766

                 South-2,013 acres
                 Buffalo Drive
                 South Park, PA 15129
                 412-835-4810 or 4809 or 5710

Web: www.alleghenycounty.us/parks

Support local crafters at the Covered Bridge Festival.

The Covered Bridge Festival offers a sample of the crafts, food, and engaging entertainment that attract visitors each year during the third weekend in September. Though there are 10 locations, the Ebenezer Bridge draws the most visitors. Food and snacks abound but homemade pie from Spring House is tough to beat. See the website for details.

shop   food   activity

Where: Washington County
                Chamber of Commerce
                375 Southpointe Blvd, Suite 240
                Canonsburg, PA 15317

                Alternate reference:
                Mingo Creek Park
                (GPS N40 11.51 W80 02.41)

Web: www.visitwashingtoncountypa.com
                www.pacoveredbridges.com

Spend an autumn day in the Allegheny Mountains at Frank Lloyd Wright's Fallingwater.

In the 1930s, architect Frank Lloyd Wright designed a mountain retreat over a waterfall. The house was for the Kaufmann family, who owned the Pittsburgh-based department store of the same name (now known as Macy's). The original mountain retreat was no more than a cabin on a country road but the Frank Lloyd Wright design is known worldwide. Fallingwater offers tours every month except January and February and reservations are needed.

culture   activity

Where: Fallingwater
                1491 Mill Run Road
                Mill Run, PA 15464
                724-329-8501

Web: www.fallingwater.org/66

Crawl through the caves, or trek with a guide, at Laurel Caverns near the Summit Inn Resort.

Three miles of passages, most with ceilings from ten to twenty feet high and average widths of twelve feet, offer visitors an underground playground in the largest cave in Pennsylvania. Guided one hour tours, cave rappelling, cave enclosed miniature golf, and spelunking are available to visitors. Temperatures are constant at 52 degrees. Laurel Caverns is open daily except during bat hibernation season (November through April). See the website for details as there are different requirements for each activity.

activity

Where: Laurel Caverns
                Hopwood, PA 15445
                Atop Chestnut Ridge
                GPS not accurate

Web: www.laurelcaverns.com

Rest and restore at the Summit Inn Resort or try a stay in the Treehouse Bungalow.

The Summit Inn Resort is perched above Uniontown and is situated on 1200 acres near Fallingwater, Laurel Caverns, and Ohiopyle. Originally built by the millionaires from nearby Uniontown, the current management is third generation and has managed to combine historic ambiance with modern amenities such as the new Treehouse Bungalow.

view   activity

Where: The Summit Inn Resort
                101 Skyline Drive
                Farmington, PA 15437
                724-438-8594 or 1-800-433-8594
                Open April - November

Web: www.summitinnresort.com

Test the currents and whitewater at Ohiopyle.

Ohiopyle State Park is comprised of approximately 20,000 acres of land on the Laurel Ridge which is located near Uniontown. One of the main attractions is whitewater rafting on the "Yawk" or Youghiogheny River. Guided tours are available and recommended. For the less adventuresome, the park offers 27 miles of flat, crushed limestone biking trails as well as camping, hiking, horseback riding, backpacking, rollerblading, fishing, rock climbing, boating, and swimming.

activity

Where: Ohiopyle
             P.O. Box 105 (Off PA 381 South)
             Ohiopyle, PA 15470
             724-329-8591
             ohiopylesp@pa.gov

Web: www.dcnr.state.pa.us/stateparks

Give thanks to those who gave their lives on 9/11 by visiting the Flight 93 memorial in Shanksville.

United Airlines Flight 93 was scheduled to travel from Newark to San Francisco on September 11, 2001 when hijackers took control of the Boeing 757 and redirected it toward Washington, D.C. The thirty-three passengers and seven crew members perished after hijackers opted to crash the jet in lieu of losing control of the plane. The first elements of the memorial were dedicated and opened on September 10, 2011.

view

activity

Where: 6424 Lincoln Highway
                   Storystown, PA 15563
                   814-893-6322

Web: www.nps.gov/flni

Celebrate Scottish tradition at the Ligonier Highland Games.

The bag pipes, kilts, harps, dancing, sheep, dogs, story-telling, food, and athletic competitions transport visitors to Scotland each September. The Ligonier Highland Games have celebrated Scottish heritage and tradition for over 55 years and are one of 30+ cities in the United States to host such games. Tradition abounds.

culture   activity

Where: Route 30
                Ligonier, PA
                1-814-931-4714

Web: www.ligonierhighlandgames.org
                www.asgf.org

Sample the outdoors at Deer Valley (DV) YMCA Camp.

Deer Valley YMCA Camp operates all year and offers special themed weekends as well as summer family camp weeks. Various types of cabin lodging provide for the basic necessities but a full-time dining staff adds the comfort food. Campfires, sailing, hiking, crafts, horseback riding, and zip lining offer the rest. Adults and kids often see each other once a year during a DV summer week but many form lifelong bonds with peers despite very limited wi-fi on the mountain. See the website for more details. Space is limited.

activity   view

Where: Deer Valley YMCA
            254 Deer Valley Drive
            Fort Hill, PA 15540
            1-800-YMCA-FUN

Web: www.deervalleyymca.org

Bike from Pittsburgh to Washington, D.C.

The Great Allegheny Passage (GAP) is primarily built on crushed limestone and is used by bikers, hikers, and other outdoor enthusiasts. The GAP extends 335 continuous miles from Pittsburgh, PA to Cumberland, MD where it connects to the C & O Canal and continues to Washington, D.C. See maps for details.

activity

Where: Allegheny Trail Alliance (ATA)
           Latrobe, PA 15650
           888-282-BIKE

           Rails-to-Trails Conservancy
           2121 Ward Ct., NW – 5th floor
           Washington, D.C. 20037
           202-331-9696

Web: www.atatrail.org
           www.railstotrails.org

More about the Bucket List series

The series originated with *The Key West Bucket List* by David Sloan. His work and guidance evolved from that original text to:

The Ocean City New Jersey Bucket List, by
Mary Ann Bolan

The Tennessee Bucket List, by Michael Crisp.

The Ohio Bucket List, by Michael Crisp.

The Kentucky Bucket List, by Michael Crisp.

The Newburyport, Massachusetts Bucket List, by Chris Johnston, Sheila Bridgland, & Jessamyn Anderson.

The Wisconsin Bucket List, by Kelly Jo Stull.

Made in the USA
Charleston, SC
19 August 2014